Star Angel
A Story of Peace

By Janet A. Slusser

Unless otherwise indicated, all Scripture quotations are taken from the *King James Version* of the Bible.

ISBN 0692582053

ISBN 9780692582053

In loving memory of my sister Sue, the best sister in the world.

Contents

Foreword

STAR ANGEL is for anyone suffering a great loss—whether that loss be a loved one, a relationship, a job, a lifestyle, or any cause—mourning that which used to be. It is also the story of one woman's search for Christmas spirit and the joyful celebration of God's wonderful gift to humanity.

It is my sincere hope that anyone going through the grief process will find hope and comfort in STAR ANGEL. May you, dear reader, find your own special Star Angel to lead you to perfect peace.

Janet A. Slusser

"A spotlight on a fresh boxwood wreath...bestowed honor to the front entry."

CHAPTER 1

Over-The-Top

Over-the-top . . . I wholeheartedly agree with that assessment of my enthusiasm for the year's biggest holiday. While friends slowly dismantle and downsize Christmas to a fraction of its former self, I cling steadfast and undaunted to my old family traditions. In truth, sometimes I wish I could minimize, strip Christmas down to the basics. Certainly, a tabletop tree, store bought treats, and gift cards would make things a lot simpler. But for me, Christmas wouldn't be Christmas without my holiday traditions. Downsize Christmas? Why, that would mean downsizing my Christmas spirit!

The journey to Christmas 2012 began the usual way. In late November, the house became the focus of a major cleaning blitz. Mops, buckets, brooms, dustpans, cleaners, and polishes of all sorts marched into formation to defend Mother's notorious words: "Christmas won't come until the whole house is clean!" Upstairs and down, the cleaning blitz went on for several days until the house was immaculate. Only one chore remained. Knowing Mother was the only housewife in the neighborhood to wash windows on the outside, even in freezing temperatures, I headed to the garage for the stepladder, another of her euphemisms echoing in my brain: "At Christmas time, if the windows are clean, the whole house sparkles!"

Once the house was scrubbed and polished, my favorite holiday predictably unfolded with precision clockwork. Fresh garland of white pine draped the threshold, and tired, rusty porch lanterns popped with red velvet bows. Frosty white lights trimmed the railed fence that outlined the long winding driveway, while reindeer and snowmen appeared on the front lawn, greeting passers by with blinking colored lights and animated smiles. A spotlight on a fresh boxwood wreath—each year adorned with Great Grandfather's tarnished but still precious sleigh bells—bestowed honor to the front entry. And finally, an eleven-foot spruce, hand picked and hand cut, soared gallantly upward through two-story windows as old-fashioned lights and cherished ornaments beckoned once more: "Come inside, friends. Inhale the aroma of fresh cut pine and hot steamy cider! It's that time of year again . . . time for a Christmas visit!"

"...old-fashioned lights and cherished ornaments..."

CHAPTER 2

Pastries and Package Ties

Christmas 2012 was right on schedule. The tree was trimmed, the yard decorated, and familiar carols echoed throughout the house. My favorite instrumentals, Vivaldi's "Winter," Corelli's "Christmas Concerto," and Handel's "Messiah," soared in the background, too—the magnificent sounds of the Masters mingling with the magnificent aromas of homemade treats.

For weeks now, I stacked the freezer with frozen pastries: sour cream coffee cakes, sticky pecan buns, cinnamon cakes, apple strudels, apricot turnovers, and most delectable of all—Aunt Esther's nut rolls—made to perfection from her prized recipes. These gifts from my kitchen were ready to bake at a moment's notice.

The week before Christmas dawned and signaled the start of a cookie baking marathon. In assembly line fashion, such delights as gingerbread men, powdered sugar snowballs, melt-in-your-mouth chocolate chippers, strawberry jam thumbprints, peanut butter blossoms, and sugar cookie cutouts (the dough enhanced by Grandmother Theresa's secret ingredient: a tablespoon of fresh lemon zest) rolled out of the oven and tumbled into brightly colored cookie tins, awaiting delivery to family and friends. Now a marathon of this nature might wear some women down, but the female members of Mother's family took all in stride. "Anyone can go to a bakery and buy Christmas goodies," Mom would say, "but we (meaning the women in our family) bake them ourselves.

That way they're extra-special and loaded with love!"

While Mother's family handed down treasured holiday recipes, Dad's family passed along a talent for design and craftsmanship. "The women in our family have been blessed with creative minds and busy hands," I heard my Great Aunt Kate say more than once. "Christmas gifts always begin as creative ideas that take shape at the sewing machine or craft table." So as not to disappoint my Aunt Kate, even though she had been gone for years now, the sewing machine was plugged in and ready to run anytime I could get away from the oven.

I carefully checked off my homemade gift list: for granddaughters—dainty glass bead bracelets nestled in voile pouches with pastel colored drawstrings; for grandsons—colorful blankets from each boy's favorite sports logo fleece; for daughters—Christmas pillows and matching Christmas tree skirts; for sons—plaid flannel scarves; for toddlers—furry brown Rudolphs with red pompom noses and plump wobbly Frostys with orange pompom noses. And finally, as "He Shall Feed His Flock" whispered like a lullaby in the background, I lovingly sewed soft, sleepy lambs for the new babies. Holiday package ties from pine cones that were gathered in the fall and home made tags from last year's Christmas cards provided the final touches. These I tucked into ribbon bows on hand wrapped boxes—no Christmas bags for my gifts!

As I placed the last present under the tree, a feeling of sweet exhaustion came over me. Christmas was near, and I had managed to keep the traditions for another year! Yes, my friends are undeniably correct. When it comes to Christmas spirit, I am and always will be "over-the-top"!

CHAPTER 3

The Nativity

Finally, Christmas Eve arrived. The tree and outside lights blinked happily, and flames in the fireplace swayed in perfect time to "What Child is This?" The living room brimmed with holiday warmth. One last thing remained to be done. I turned off the lights.

Knowing full well the real meaning of Christmas, I have a special tradition for welcoming the Christ Child. On Christmas Eve, just before midnight, I place white candles around the house and light them one by one until each darkened room flickers in candlelight. Then I place a white taper on the mantle, but it remains unlit.

By the glow of lighted candles, I make my way into the dining room to the old sideboard and open the bottom drawer. I remove a large box with bold lettering across the top. With child-like anticipation, I open the lid and remove the yellowed and crumpled tissue paper. There inside is one of my cherished possessions: a one-of-a-kind, hand-carved Nativity set.

I received these treasured pieces many years ago—a gift from the first church choir I had the pleasure of directing. One of the choir members had traveled to South America and spotted the Nativity in a small wood carver's shop in Brazil. No two carvings are the same, so my Nativity is unlike any other in the world.

This Christmas Eve, I lifted the figures carefully from the box and for several moments held each member of the Holy Family in my hands, studying subtle details as if seeing them for the first time. The beauty of the carvings is amazing. Each year I enjoy them more.

Carved from rosewood, the statue of Mary is painted in rich, intense colors. Her delicate features depict a child-like mother, perhaps no more than fourteen years old. A mantle of deep blue wraps around her, and one hand reaches tenderly for the Child. Her head tilts slightly to one side. Her face expresses both joy and bewilderment.

The statue of Joseph is a larger, heavier figure. He appears older than Mary. His body and face evoke strength, wisdom, and a subtle tenderness. His eyes are wide with wonder and kindness as he leans on a branch bearing white berries. I noticed a chip of paint missing from the brown cloak that drapes to his sandaled feet. "Hmm . . ." I said, "I wonder when this happened?" I made a mental note to touch it up before next year.

The Baby Jesus is my favorite figure. A tiny, frail infant lies in a low, rustic manger. The white swaddling cloths are unbelievably lifelike —each fold and crease etched in wood. Clumps of straw form a bedding that appears soft and perfect for a newborn baby. The face of the Savior is remarkably detailed. He sleeps blissfully under a halo of tiny hand-carved stars.

I unwrapped the animals—a cow, a donkey, and two sheep—and assembled the crude stable made of small pieces of wood. The thatch from the roof was missing in places, creating quite an open shelter. *I really should repair this*, I thought, as I carried all to the fireplace mantle and carefully arranged each piece. Once the figures were positioned, I placed the white candle beside them. I struck the match. It was time to welcome the Christ Child . . . time to celebrate His coming . . . time to allow the real spirit of Christmas to fill my heart.

I lit the candle and waited for the flame to catch the wick. This is the exciting part—watching the wick burst into flame, illuminating the figures in the dark stable. "And He will bring light unto the darkness," I whispered. "He will bring glory unto the people. Behold, the Prince of Peace." This last bit from Scripture (Luke 2:32) was the cue for my Christmas prayer, the same prayer I utter every Christmas Eve: "Thank you Father, for giving the world your only Son. May He enter my heart this Christmas season bringing peace, joy, and love everlasting."

The glow of the candlelight on the lifelike faces in the stable, the verses of Scripture, and my Christmas prayer—these are the last of my Christmas traditions. Like a giant puzzle, all pieces of Christmas had fallen into perfect position. A Son is born! Hallelujah! And Amen!

"The mantle clock chimed and startled me."

CHAPTER 4

The Star Halo

The candles flickered in the darkness: "Christ is born! Christ is born!" they proclaimed, as rays of light darted about the room like shooting stars in a midnight sky. I waited for the wave of sheer joy to rise up inside of me, that surge of Christmas spirit that flies like a spark of electricity from my head to my toes and back again. But the moment passed in awkward nothingness . . . I realized something was "off." Something didn't feel right. Something was missing. I had seen the same figures illumined year after year. I had whispered the same Scriptures, prayed the same prayer. But tonight, something was different.

I gazed at the figures in the stable for a long time. It took a while, but I finally figured out what was wrong. It was the star halo, the ring of stars that circle the head of Baby Jesus.

The star halo is a favorite detail of mine. At first glance, it appears to be a circle of thorns over the head of Jesus, but closer inspection reveals a cluster of tiny, perfectly carved stars, each one overlapping the other to form a tightly woven halo. The stars are painted with a lustrous gold paint that sparkles in the reflection of shimmering candlelight. But tonight, the halo was dim.

It must be a shadow, I thought, as I moved the candle closer. Still, the halo didn't glow. *Maybe the gold paint is wearing thin*, I reasoned, as I reached for the Baby Jesus to study the halo. *After all, these figures were given to me years ago and are starting to show some signs of age.* I inspected the halo for a moment, looking for thin places in the gold paint. The tiny stars were perfect. It was obvious that wasn't the problem. "Oh, so what if the halo doesn't shine," I said, trying to convince myself. "It's not such a big deal." I returned the figure to its spot, hoping for resolve on the issue.

But the truth of the matter—it was a big deal. Each Christmas Eve when the star halo sparkles, something stirs inside me—a wonderful, warm feeling. When I feel that warmth of Christmas spirit, I know the Prince of Peace has come—not just to the world, but to me personally—into my heart and into my life. For some reason, the feeling was missing this year, just like the glow of Christ's tiny halo of stars.

I stood staring at the star halo for several moments, as if fixating on it would cause some sparkle. The mantle clock chimed and startled me. My thoughts were interrupted. I waited for the clock to strike twelve. It was midnight—midnight on Christmas Eve.

I went to the closet and took out my coat, hat, and scarf. Each Christmas Eve I leave the comfort of my living room and head outside to imagine what it must have felt like to be a shepherd on the hills outside of Bethlehem. I opened the back door. *When I see the stars shining*, I thought, with a renewed sense of confidence, *I'll have that glow back again.*

I wrapped my scarf tightly around my neck and started across the back yard, away from the bright lights and front door spotlight. It was a cold Christmas Eve. The snow had just begun to fall, and the ground was dusted with white patches. But the month of December had been unseasonably mild. The ground was still warm, and forecasters predicted a green Christmas this year. A chilly gust of wind tousled my hair as I made my way to a row of evergreens. The pine tree boughs were just beginning to turn white from the falling snow. *How pretty they look*, I thought, *all dressed in their finest white lace*. The trees were beautiful, but I was slightly irritated.

"The pine tree boughs were just beginning to turn white..."

"For Pete's sake! It's Christmas Eve!" I shouted, a little too loudly. "Can't the snow stick . . . at least for tonight?" I was surprised at how disgruntled I sounded. How could I, of all people, be irritated on Christmas Eve? I managed to calm myself. "Oh well," I said, "the ground is warm, and that means no white Christmas this year. It's okay . . . we've celebrated many green Christmases in the past." I resigned myself to the inevitable: the snow would melt away as predicted . . . disappear . . . just like my Christmas spirit. Still, as hard as it was, I could accept a Christmas without snow easier than a Christmas without spirit.

I looked up and searched the night sky. Not a star was shining in the heavens. I could make out some clouds, low and motionless; but even the clouds were hard to see. It was just too dark. "Too much cloud cover tonight," I muttered. "How can I pretend to be a shepherd when there isn't a star in the sky?" I stood for a moment, trying as hard as I could to imagine the night of the Savior's birth . . . *And there were in the same country shepherds abiding in the field, keeping watch over their flock by night. And lo, the angel of the Lord came upon them, and the glory of the Lord shone round about them* . . . (Luke 2:8-9 KJV) Nothing. It was no use.

The wonder, fear, amazement, joy, anticipation . . . emotions that surely overwhelmed the shepherds . . . well, I simply couldn't feel any of these. I was just someone standing in the backyard on a cold December night, watching the snow melt . . . someone looking for twinkling stars in a black sky . . . someone who had immersed herself in all the traditions of Christmases past: the immaculate house, the sleigh bell wreath, the eleven-foot tree, Aunt Esther's nut rolls, the homemade gifts, the candles. But I couldn't seem to experience the immeasurable, unspeakable joy of God's gift in the present. I was someone who used to be filled with Christmas spirit, but I couldn't seem to find it this year. Instead, I was someone consumed by immeasurable grief and unspeakable sadness. Of course, I knew why I felt this way.

CHAPTER 5

My Sister Sue

Five months before this Christmas, my sister died. She was diagnosed a year and a half earlier with a rare and terminal disease. The months leading up to her death were devastating as I watched a beautiful woman who lived life with such energy and enthusiasm slowly weaken and wither away.

My sister Sue was a huge part of my life. Being three years younger than Sue, she was always my role model. From the day I was born, she was there, and I wanted to be exactly like her. So I copied what she did and imitated the manner in which she did it. From the way she wore her hair to the instrument she played in the school orchestra, I was a carbon copy. I even attended the same college. The amazing thing is that Sue never appeared angry or disgusted with me for trying to be like her. That wasn't how she was wired. My sister was an exceptional human being, and she influenced me more than any other person on earth.

Sue loved God, and she loved people. Her life's work—a career in the ministry—was a perfect fit. Sue loved to talk, and she had an amazing and positive way with words. She knew what people needed to hear. She knew what to say and how to say it. My sister was also a great judge of character. She had a keen way of sizing people up and building them up. In a few moments of conversation, she could sense what strength or weakness someone might have. Then, before you knew it, she would work her magic: The weakness would vanish, and the strength would seem even greater. In her presence, people felt stronger and better because, somehow, she always brought out the best.

As hard as I tried, I couldn't imitate my sister's wonderful, outgoing personality. She had an easy-going charm and friendly, genuine manner that made her popular with girlfriends, boyfriends, teachers, mentors . . . everyone. Sue had a gift—a zest for life—and people gravitated toward her, hoping this enthusiasm would rub off. In reality, Sue herself was the gift. And people loved her.

"...I wanted to be exactly like her."

It didn't take long to realize I wasn't the "people" person my beautiful older sister was. I was more comfortable in front of a music stand than socializing with others. I outgrew the insecurities of childhood days, but I never felt that I measured up to the sister I adored. Even as adults, I often hovered in the background while Sue, with her beautiful smile, twinkling dark eyes, and radiant personality, captivated everyone in the room.

"Sue began calling me Honey Bun a long time ago."

CHAPTER 6

Honey Bun

Sue had a pet name for her favorite people. You knew you were special if she called you "Honey Bun." Now, I don't know where, why, or when this began, but once you got used to being called Honey Bun, Sue could get you to do just about anything! I remember a phone call she made to a parishioner: "Hi, Honey Bun! I've just heard some WONDERFUL news! YOU are a WONDER when it comes to NUMBERS! And we just happen to be looking for SOMEONE to chair the FINANCE committee. Now isn't that a MARVELOUS coincidence? OH, I know you've got a million things on your plate, but you WILL consider joining us, won't you . . . Honey Bun?" Bingo! I knew that person was on board whether he or she wanted to be or not! My sister could work a room, and she could work a church member, too!

Sue began calling me Honey Bun a long time ago. If I visited her at home in Pittsburgh, she greeted me at the door with a hug and a kiss and a whisper in my ear, "Hi, Honey Bun . . . GREAT to see you." If I called on the phone, I expected to hear, "Honey Bun, so GOOD of you to call." Or, "Honey Bun, how ARE you?" as if we hadn't spoken to each other for years!

After my sister was diagnosed with cancer, my visits became more frequent. My calls multiplied. In the last months of her life, I visited as often as I could and called each day. At first, her "Honey Bun" greetings were strong and heartfelt. But as she grew weaker and wearier, so were her salutations. I could always tell how she was feeling by the way she said Honey Bun. At the end, calls were short and abrupt. She was too weak to hold the phone. "Honey Bun" was barely audible.

I was with my sister the evening she passed away. I drove to her home for a visit that night. She was bedridden now, and I expected that she would be weak and tired, but I had no idea how frail she had become. It was a hot July day. I entered her bedroom. I nearly started the conversation with "How are you?" but stopped myself when I saw how small she looked, lying under one white sheet. She had lost more weight. The cancer had emaciated my sister almost beyond recognition. Clearly, "How are you?" was not the right thing to ask.

I walked toward the window. The blinds were opened enough to reveal the tops of lilies in the outside garden. "Oh, Sue," I said, trying desperately to sound cheery, "the lilies are lovely! Can you see them?" She was lying on her side. I hoped she was looking at the flowers. We had planted them together last spring. I could remember every detail about that day.

"The blinds were opened enough to reveal the tops of lilies..."

~

It was late April. The sun's warm rays had sliced through the chilly morning mist. It was a perfect spring morning . . . fresh, warm, and bright. My phone rang at 7:30 a.m. It was Sue.

"Hi, Honey Bun," she said with her usual enthusiasm. "What a gorgeous day! Would you like to come over and help me plant a lily garden? I thought we might loosen the soil under the bedroom window. That area gets quite a bit of sun. I bought all colors of bulbs. It will be a beautiful garden . . . a memorial garden."

Of course I said "yes."

I made the two hour trip to her home. Sue didn't answer the front doorbell. I figured she was out back, so I walked around the side yard. Bits of purple and yellow appeared on the hillside behind Sue's patio . . . daffodils and crocuses lifting their tiny blossomed faces to the brightness. "First harbingers of spring," I thought out loud. Sue was already hard at work, cleaning out the garden beds. She had gotten the shovels, hoes, wheelbarrow, and garden gloves out for us. I smiled as I looked at the tools: "Ah, and of course, there are the second harbingers of spring."

The sunshine had energized Sue. I felt a surge of energy, too, because I knew she was having a "good" day. We exchanged our hellos, and I got right to work. I dug into the earth under the bedroom window and lifted shovelfuls of dirt to the surface. Sue busted up the big clumps with the toes of her garden boots, saying "take that!" with every kick. I went over the smaller clumps with the hoe. Finally the soil was smooth and ready to plant.

We were weeding as we went along and talking and laughing about everything imaginable. After a while, we realized we were exhausted. The fact that we sisters were not at all used to this much physical labor had worn us out. "We'd better take a break," Sue said.

She fetched the lawn chairs and fixed us some lemonade. I made holes in the garden for the lily bulbs. We sipped our drinks and enjoyed the moment. Sue reached for a bag of bulbs. "Look at these things!" she said, referring to the picture of beautiful lilies on the package label. "They're absolutely dazzling!" Sue finished her lemonade and stood up. "I'll go first and toss one of these 'puppies' into a hole. You follow with the shovel and cover them with dirt. Before long the root hairs will creep out; stems will poke up; leaves will appear; and finally, in July, these gorgeous lilies will be mine!" I hadn't seen her this excited for some time.

But her enthusiasm faded. She grew quiet. I knew what she was thinking. The situation was full of irony. The bulbs would lie in the earth until the roots could anchor the plant and suck the life giving minerals and water into the shoots. In a matter of weeks, leaves would sprout, then blossoms, opening to reveal the vibrant flowers. At the same time, cancer cells would grow and multiply inside Sue's body draining her energy from within. The lilies would grow strong and prosper, but Sue would become weaker and more ill. When the lilies were in full splendor, she would be bedridden, waiting to die. We didn't say anything; we just held each other and allowed ourselves to cry unashamed. "It will be a beautiful memorial garden," she whispered.

~

I walked around to where I could see her face. She was asleep. Even close to death, she was beautiful. Her hair curled softly around her face, and I was immediately thankful she hadn't lost it in chemo treatments. Her face was colorless, but her skin still had the soft texture of a woman much younger. She lay still with only an occasional breath. Her eyelids fluttered. "Sue, I whispered, "it's me. I'm here."

I knelt down beside the bed and took her hand. Suddenly, years and years of memories flashed before my eyes. Here was the person who shared my life from the day I was born. Here was my first playmate and the one who walked me to school hand in hand. Here was the girl who taught me to ride a bike and then bandaged my skinned knees. Here was the teenager who allowed me to tag along with her friends, never pushing me aside. Here was my confidant in high school, my mentor in college, and my "go to" person throughout my adult life. Here was my closest sibling, my sister, my dearest, sweetest friend. She had been my role model for everything. And now, having fought the most difficult battle of her life with grace and dignity and courage, she was my hero. I loved her deeply and couldn't bear the thought of never hearing her voice again, of losing her forever. I buried my face in her hair and wept uncontrollably.

"Susie, Susie, my beautiful, dear sister," I sobbed. "Please don't die. I can't lose you. I love you so very much." She tried to reach for my hand, but the gesture was too much for her. She labored to speak. "Honey Bun," she barely whispered, "come, lie down with me." I eased into the bed, knowing the slightest motion could cause her pain. I held her gently in my arms and, between sobs, thanked her for being the best sister anyone could have. Over and over I told her I loved her until the tears choked my words, and there was nothing more to say. She tried to squeeze my hand with her last bit of strength. "Don't cry," she whispered. "Be at peace with this. I am. Please, let God fill you with perfect peace. It's alright, Honey Bun. It's going to be alright."

I held my sister for a long time until she fell asleep again. Then, I laid her head gently on the pillow. I left the room grief stricken and trembling. Sue died an hour later.

CHAPTER 7

She Opened the Bag

A gust of wind brought me back to reality. I was shivering in the frigid air. "Just too much cloud cover tonight," I said, disappointed. I turned to go inside. "Perhaps next Christmas Eve there will be some stars. . ."

Swoosh! I heard a noise above my head. It sounded like air moving. A faint light appeared in the darkness. Then, swoosh again. "Oh, pardon me," a small voice said. "I can't seem to get the hang of these things. My goodness, it's dark! I'm so sorry I'm late."

I noticed a dimly lit figure high above me. The clouds were barely visible, but they seemed to swirl around the small being. Then I saw feathers . . . and wings . . . and what appeared to be a large cloth bag. The bag was as large as the figure. I could hardly believe my eyes. It was an angel!

"What's there?" I called out in the darkness. "Who are you?" I wasn't at all frightened by the figure, just surprised. "Oh my, where are my manners?" said the angel. "Please, allow me to introduce myself. I am a Star Angel. I'm one of many starry host responsible for lighting up the heavens tonight. As you can see, I've done a terrible job." She paused, as if searching for an explanation. "I know I'm new here and just learning the ropes. But truthfully, I haven't gotten used to these things yet!" She motioned to her wings. "I just got these contraptions, and they're not as easy as people think. I'm trying to be very cautious until I learn how to use them correctly."

She seemed to emphasize some words more than others. It made listening to her easy and pleasant. I was thinking about this when the Star Angel came closer. She flew down slowly and landed carefully and precisely on the ground, right next to where I was standing. Her bag seemed cumbersome and landed with a heavy THUG! "Made it!" she said, "even with this heavy sack. It's got to weigh a ton!" she sighed. "But I can take care of that." She opened the bag and light filtered out. Slowly at first, then rushing full force to the skies until the heavens were filled with millions of gleaming stars. "Now that's more like it," she said, brushing her palms together, obviously pleased with herself. "I always say, better late than never!"

I stood there with my mouth wide open! The sky had gone from pitch black to brilliant light in a matter of seconds! "Wow!" I said. "So this is what the shepherds saw over Bethlehem. Awesome." She smiled. "Come out here often, do you? To stargaze?" "Well . . . um . . ." I stammered, not wanting to tell her I was pretending to be a shepherd for fear she'd think me silly. "Mainly on Christmas Eve. It's just something I do."

I noticed the starlight shining on her face. She was really quite a sweet little angel. I wondered if she could tell I was a bit embarrassed about my last statement. Then a beautiful smile came over her face. "Helps to put you in the Christmas spirit, doesn't it?" she said. Before I could answer, she continued on. "You know, you look like someone who could use a couple of glad tidings." I watched as she knelt down and put her hand deep into the bag. She reached around in the bottom for a few seconds and brought out a handful of white powdered starlight. "Here you go," she said, as she sprinkled some over me. "I use this a lot on people. It always seems to help."

The white powder fell gently over my body. I began to feel a little light-headed and heard myself giggle for the first time in months. "Thanks," I said. "Yes, I need a couple of these for sure. You see . . ." I was doubled over with laughter now and suddenly burst into song at full voice: "Oh glad tidings . . . sweet glad tidings . . . powdered bits of starlight . . . just a fallin' over me!" I hurried and put my hand over my mouth. My jubilant song was echoing over the hillside! "Gosh, what's IN that stuff?" I asked, as I regained my composure. "I don't think I've laughed that hard or belted out a song like that since before my sister . . ."

I didn't finish my thought. I didn't have to. It seemed as if the Star Angel already knew what I intended to say. She nodded her head and smiled. Her dark eyes filled with kindness. "Well," said the Star Angel, as a matter-of-fact, "it's officially Christmas, and I do have places I need to be. I suppose I had better move along now." She knelt down to gather her empty sack. She looked up but hesitated before standing. "However, there is something I should do before I leave. Do you have your Nativity scene on display? If you do, I must make sure the star is shining . . . that is, if you have a star." She stood up now and proceeded to tie the bag closed. "You know, many people on earth don't realize there are lots of jobs to be done in heaven." She went on, eager to explain. "We angels have work to do. Keeping the Nativity star polished and shining brightly over every Christ Child figure is one of those important jobs . . . indeed, an honor."

She lowered her voice to a whisper now and winked at me. "I think 'You-Know-Who' was pleased with my work when I lived on earth. Some angels have to wait years to land something like this. I haven't lived in heaven very long. Kind of makes me feel special." I nodded and smiled. I had to agree. She was special. I liked her a lot, even though we just met.

I was suddenly excited to show the Star Angel my treasured figures. I couldn't wait to tell her about my candlelight tradition and my Christmas prayer. But mostly, I wanted to see if she could put some sparkle into the star halo. "I have a hand-carved Nativity that I place on the mantle each Christmas. It's my favorite decoration, but the star halo over the Baby Jesus could certainly use your attention. Please, do come inside and see it!" "Oh, I can work just fine through the window," she said, "but perhaps you should go inside now. Just look at the snow falling!" She turned her palms up so I could see the snowflakes gathering there. "Brr . . . it's freezing out here!" She pulled her robe tightly around her shoulders and gave me another smile. I could see that her eyes were twinkling. "Go on," she said. "I'll meet you at the window."

I nodded and hurried to the front door. As I turned the knob, I looked over my shoulder to see if she had flown to the window. I was surprised to see her right there behind me. Her hands were cupped with soft blue powdered starlight. I turned around just in time to see her sprinkle the blue softness over my head.

CHAPTER 8

A Christmas Present

"Hey, what's this?" I asked. "More glad tidings of great joy?" Her smile faded. She was serious now. "No, not glad tidings. Something much more important than that." She extended her hand toward me. "This blue starlight is peace . . . peace on earth. I felt you needed some of that, too. Consider it a present . . . a Christmas present . . . from me to you."

I didn't know what to say. In truth, I was startled to see the blue powder on my coat and scarf. She waited for my response, her hand still outstretched. "You know," she said kindly, "a present is something given and received. You will accept my gift, won't you?" She was imploring only for an instant. Then, she smiled that beautiful smile again, and for the first time since my sister's death, a strange but wonderful calmness came over me.

I couldn't explain what had happened, but my heart was light and open. Gone was the grief that so heavily weighed it down. Gone was the sorrow so tightly locked inside. Somehow, I released the grief and sorrow and, in doing so, created space for something else. The Star Angel filled the void with her amazing gift. She replaced the crippling sadness with the unspeakable, perfect peace of God. And finally, after months of suffering the loss of my beloved Sue, I allowed myself to accept it. Thanks to the Star Angel's gift, I felt free and unburdened. I was ready to move past Sue's death . . . to move on . . . to move forward . . . to enjoy living my life once again.

Suddenly, without warning, a wave of sheer joy—that surge of Christmas spirit that flies like a spark of electricity from my head to my toes and back again—rose up inside me. A warm and wonderful feeling rushed over my body. It was the awesomeness of a Baby born long ago in a filthy, dusty stable. It was the wonder of God's amazing love for a darkened sorrowful world. It was the Peace that passes understanding, filling me up with hope and a sense of new life. It was the joy of Christmas! I had found my Christmas spirit!

CHAPTER 9

Peace on Earth

I opened the door. The Christmas candles were still burning in the darkened room. I walked to the mantle and peered at the Nativity figures. There was Mary, kneeling beside the Child, and Joseph, his eyes wide with wonder. I reached for the Baby Jesus and held the figure in my hand. "Here is the Son of God," I whispered. "The greatest gift mankind will ever know." And then a wonderful thing happened . . . the tiny halo of perfectly carved stars began to glow. It began softly at first, and then grew stronger and more brilliant until its beam of light shone brighter than all the lighted white candles put together.

I looked to the living room window. The Star Angel was peeking inside. Her cherub face had the sweetest grin I've ever seen. I returned her smile with one of my own—one that said, "Thank you for the star halo and its sparkle, but most of all, for filling me with peace on earth. Thank you. I am at peace." The Star Angel lingered a moment. She seemed to be waiting for something. I walked to the window with the baby Jesus in my hand and waved good bye and blew her a kiss. Her brown eyes twinkled as she waved back at me and mouthed the words "Merry Christmas, Honey Bun."

"I opened the window."

CHAPTER 10

A Merry Christmas

It was snowing hard now. The forecasters had been wrong. The ground was covered with sparkling white snow—snow that was sticking to the ground. Snow that would last throughout the Christmas season. I opened the window. The freezing cold of that Christmas Eve night rushed into the warmth of the living room, stinging my face and nearly extinguishing the candles. But I didn't care. For peace, joy, and everlasting love filled my heart with a warm glow that would stick like the snow outside and not melt away.

I watched the Star Angel float upwards, the empty bag still in her hands. As she disappeared into the starry glow of heaven, I spoke these words from the second chapter of Luke with joyous conviction: "And there were in the same country shepherds abiding in the field, keeping watch over their flock by night. And lo, the angel of the Lord came upon them, and the glory of the Lord shone round about them." (Luke 2:8-9 KJV)

The sky was aglow now with millions of radiant stars, all twinkling down from above. But none twinkled as brightly as the Star Angel's eyes. I looked to the tiny figure in my hands; the star halo sparkled. It was never more brilliant than on this night! My heart was over-the-top with Christmas spirit, real Christmas spirit as I whispered

"Merry Christmas to you, too, my precious sister."

www.ingramcontent.com/pod-product-compliance
Lightning Source LLC
Chambersburg PA
CBHW041755050426
42443CB00023B/11